Catawba ConvertiCoops
DIY Chicken Ark Plans

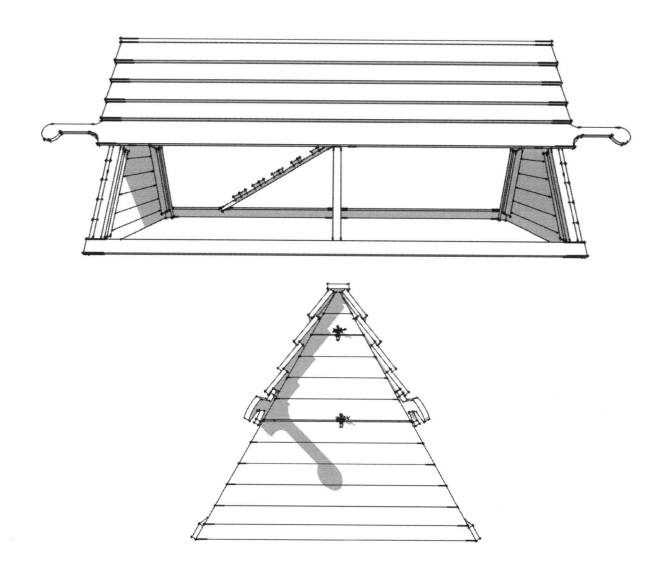

To my dad, George Bissette,
who thought that having chickens would be
a great character building experience for his son.

Copyright © 2008-2010 by David P. Bissette
All rights reserved
www.CatawbaCoops.com

Introduction

A Hard Learned Lesson

Several days before Hurricane David wound a path of destruction and havoc through the eastern coast of the US in 1979, my dad brought home a small flock of chickens. He told me these were special chickens.

Rather than laying plain old white or brown eggs, these "Easter Egg" chickens would lay eggs that were blue or green, and sometimes even pink. I thought it was the coolest thing ever.

In the fourth grade, my love of chickens had progressed to the point that I wrote a poem.

> *I have some special chickens.*
> *Ameraucanas[1] are their breed*
> *The five I have are pretty birds.*
> *They are my task to feed.*
>
> *Tex here, he's my rooster.*
> *His spurs are sharp and long.*
> *He leads his flock in search of food,*
> *And chants his chicken song.*
>
> *You ask me why they're special?*
> *Well, I'll tell you what I think.*
> *My four hens don't lay white eggs.*
> *They lay green, and blue, and pink.*

A cross stitch picture my mother made when I was younger. c. 1982

As a kid, I learned a lot from keeping chickens. Since I was solely responsible for the upkeep of the birds, I had to ensure that my chickens had fresh water and feed, even on the cold days when their water was frozen solid.

One Saturday every month, I had the unenviable task of clean-

---

1 *I found out later that my special chickens were actually a mutt breed of chicken known as "Easter Eggers". True Ameraucanas lay blue or slate colored eggs and are generally rare.*

ing out under the chicken coop. Dad would put the manure in the compost pile.

Keeping chickens was also my first experience dealing with the sensitive topic of death. Something that my parents didn't explain to me was that there's a reason why everything tastes "just like chicken." It's because everything in the woods seems to enjoy eating them. Raccoons, skunks, snakes, opossums, and the neighbor's dogs all had their eyes on my chicken flock.

One day I came home from school to find the chicken coop empty. There was nothing there; no hens, no rooster, no feathers. I was completely dumbstruck. I found a very traumatized rooster in a cardboard box in the basement.

When my mom got home from the grocery store, she told me that the neighbor's mongrel dog had gotten into the pen and killed all the hens just for sport. Worried about how I would handle it, she cleaned up all evidence of the crime. I didn't get the opportunity to say goodbye to my special chickens. I think that's what made me the saddest about losing them.

Kids don't have to be insulated from the way things are. I learned several good life lessons that day. I found out the hard way that chickens are at the bottom of the food pyramid, and death is the natural and inevitable consequence of life.

Additionally, I learned that chicken wire is very good at keeping chickens in, but very bad at keeping dogs out.

30 years later, the memories of my special chickens is still intact. I have three children of my own now. We live one block from downtown and the former Wake Forest College, in the heart of our town's historic district.

Short of selling the house and moving to the country, how could my wife and I have urban chickens in a town with regulations and laws about the keeping of livestock inside the town limits?

This manual is about how we did it.

How Us City Slickers Got Chickens Two Blocks From Town Hall

My house was built in the mid 1940's by my great-grandfather. Rev. I.T. Stroud picked a prime location for his new house. It was near the public pool which was recently built by Franklin Roosevelt's Work Projects Administration. My great-grandfather joked that WPA stood for "We piddle around."

The location was also less than 200 feet away from the Colonial Club dormitory. My great-grandmother Etta Stroud was headmistress for Wake Forest College athletes like Arnold Palmer. The dorm is now the parking lot for the Community House.

In short, when the house was finished in 1947, it was within walking distance of everything that was worth seeing in this little college town of Wake Forest.

When Mitzi and I decided that we wanted to get urban chickens, we knew that we would not be able to utilize the age old proverb that "out of sight is out of mind." In our location, there is no out of sight to make out of mind. If we were going to keep chickens we would have to follow the letter of the law when it came to the keeping of domestic livestock.

Keeping the Letter of the Law

Depending on where you live, you may choose to skip this chapter and get right to building your chicken ark. If you live out yonder in the county, you won't have to deal with the bureaucracy of getting a livestock permit.

Your city, like our neighbor city Raleigh, may not have any regulations for or against the keeping of livestock. That's wonderful news! On the other hand, if you do live in an area that requires a permit, read on friend.

So does or doesn't your city have chicken regulations? I've found an excellent resource online at ***http://www.municode.com***. This web site has the municipal ordinances for over 120 North Carolina cities alone. Just choose your state and area. A whole bevy of mind numbing rules and regulations are at your fingertips. Chapter 6, Article II, Division 2 of our local town ordinance reads:

*Sec. 6-51. Required. No person shall stable, tie or otherwise keep within the town, **nearer than 500 feet** to any dwelling house, apartment or other residence occupied by any person, without first obtaining a permit in writing signed by the town and issued as provided in this division, any of the following types of animals: Cattle; Horses; Mules; Swine; Sheep; Goats; **or Fowl**. (Code 1985, § 3-26)*

A 500 foot radius covers a long way. That's over 3 football fields in diameter. It's apparent that we're going to need a permit since we have neighbors within 500 feet of our house. But it's not as simple as just going to the permitting office and applying.

*Sec. 6-52. Application. Any person desiring to obtain a permit required by this division shall apply for such permit in writing to the town. Such application shall state the type and number of animals to be stabled, pastured, tied or otherwise kept; the places such animals will be stabled, pastured, tied or otherwise kept; the **name of one adult occupant**, if any, of each dwelling house, apartment or residence within 500 feet of such place, and **the distance of each dwelling** house, apartment or other residence from such place. (Code 1985, § 3-27)*

If we read this correctly, we just need to tell the city how many chickens we want to keep, and make a list of the heads of household for all our neighbors within a 500 feet radius of our house. And we need to figure out how far away they are too. Oy! The great thing is that we don't have to worry about businesses, stores, colleges & universities, etc. since they are not occupied dwelling houses, apartments, or residences.

Sec. 6-53. Fee. Each applicant for a permit required by this division shall pay to the town the currently required fee for each separate application, which fee shall be paid into the general fund of the town. (Code 1985, § 3-28)

In our case, it is an annual $35.00 that we had to pay into the general coffers for the privilege of keeping urban chickens. Here's where things now start to get a little sticky.

*Sec. 6-54. Approval. Upon determining that a proper application has been filed and that the fee has been paid, and upon finding that the stabling, pasturing, tying or otherwise keeping of such animals in the place stated in the application **will not endanger the health of any person** occupying a dwelling house, apartment or residence within 500 feet of such place, or any other citizen or inhabitant of the town, the town shall issue a permit specifying the number and type of animals to be stabled, pastured, tied or kept, and the places such animals may be stabled, pastured, tied or kept;*

*Provided, the town may accept as proof that such stabling, pasturing, tying or otherwise keeping of such animals in such places will not endanger the health of any person occupying a dwelling house, apartment or residence within 500 feet of such place, **the written assent to the issuance of such permit signed by one adult occupant** of each such dwelling, apartment, or other residence then occupied by human beings within 500 feet of the place such animals are to be stabled, pastured, tied or otherwise kept. (Code 1985, § 3-28)*

Of course it couldn't be as simple as just making a list of our neighbors and the distance from their house to ours. According to this section, before we can get approval from the town, we'll have to get written approval from all our neighbors.

It's time to canvas the neighborhood, drumming up support for our pet chickens and pet project.

Sec. 6-55. Period; revocation. Each permit issued by the town as provided in this division shall be and remain valid until January 1 next following the issuance of the permit, or until revoked as provided in this section. At any time within 30 days before the expiration of any permit, the permit holder may apply for renewal of such permit, which renewal shall be issued upon the same conditions as provided for the issuance of the original permit. Such renewal shall be valid for one year from the expiration of the former permit.

Such permit shall be revoked upon a finding by the town that the sta-

bling, pasturing, tying or otherwise keeping of any animal described in the permit application at the places described in the permit application endangers the health or safety of any person occupying a dwelling house, apartment or residence within 500 feet of such place, or any other citizen or inhabitants of the town. Such revocation shall be effective ten days after the mailing by registered or certified mail of a notice thereof to the last known address of the holder of the permit. (Code 1985, § 3-30)

This section makes sense to me. This is what I refer to as the escape hatch clause. That's how we pitched it to our neighbors at least. It gives them some sense of veto power in the event that we accidentally get a batch of roosters from the hatchery instead of hens, or if our chickens are running rampant through their garden.

By the way, do yourself and your neighbors a favor by giving away or cooking any roosters you may accidentally receive if you live in the city.

Who Are the People in Your Neighborhood?

Our next step was to determine how many people we had to contact. Chances are that you don't know some of the people that live nearly two football fields away from you. Neither did we. For us to find this information we turned back to the world's largest source of information, the Internet.

According to the ordinance, we had to contact everyone within 500 feet of our house. The question now arose, "500 feet from where?"

Do we calculate the radius from our front door? From the center of our property? From the place where we thought we would keep the chickens? That's a difference of over 50 feet.

In the end, we literally read the ordinance to mean *"in the place where the foul are to be kept."* This actually made it easier for us since it eliminated two households from our petition.

We're going to utilize the power of Google's freeware offerings to determine the proper distance and radius. In addition to a fine search engine, they produce some really neat pieces of free software. Google SketchUp is the software used to develop the 3 dimensional views of the chicken coop in this instruction manual.

Google Earth is another free program that allows you to fly around the globe from your home computer. Google Maps does something similar to Google Earth, but without the freedom to move around on the planet's surface that Google Earth offers.

Our first step towards making a map of our neighborhood was to pinpoint the location of the chicken coop at ***http://maps.google.com***. You can get an exact latitude and longitude by clicking the link in the upper right that reads *Link to this page*. It's going to give you a long web address.

http://maps.google.com/?ie=UTF8&
ll=35.97797,-78.512824
&spn=0.000509,0.001125&t=h&z=20

We only need the two numbers that come after *ll=*. That means *latitude* and *longitude*. The exact location on the surface of the earth where we wanted to place our chicken coop is 35.97797 degree latitude, -78.512824 degrees longitude.

Download and install Google Earth Free from ***http://earth.google.com***. Google Earth gives us the opportunity to create overlays that can be placed directly onto the surface of the Earth.

We're going to use a web site call KML Circle Generator to create a 152.4 meter radius circle overlay with a center point of our backyard where the chickens will be. In case you're wondering, 152.4 meters is 500 feet.

I could give you a long web address to type in, but it's easier to just run a Google search for *KML Circle Generator* and click on the first link. Type your information into the circle generator and click the *Go* button. Save your KML circle file somewhere on your computer's hard drive. Put it where you'll remember it. *My Documents* or on your computer's Desktop is always a good place.

Double click the KML circle file to open the file. Google Earth will open the KML file and place a red circle with a 500 foot radius around your coop location. Now you know who you need to contact. If their house doesn't fall on or inside the circle, don't worry about contacting them.

Google Earth also let us give the town an additional tidbit they were requesting; the distance in feet from the chicken coop to the neighbor's house. This is cool! Using the *Ruler Tool*, we measured from the coop location to each house's front door. In the example on the next page, our neighbor's front door is 180.09 feet from where we want to keep the chickens.

The name of the game is documentation.

Remember that rules and ordinances are in place to keep a few unorthodox people governed. Local officials and bureaucrats are not there to make your life difficult. They have the unenviable posi-

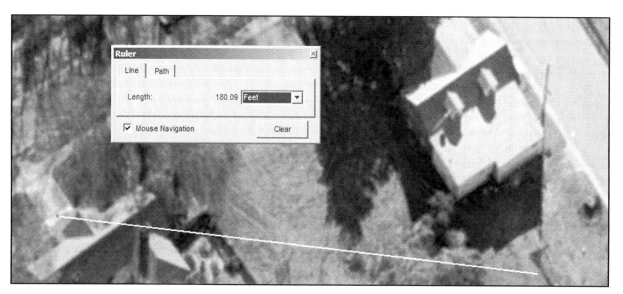

tion of ensuring that everyone in the community plays nicely with each other. Your job is to document your actions completely and thoroughly so town officials know that both you and all your urban neighbors are in agreement about the decision to keep chickens in your backyard.

Marketing 101

The foundation of marketing is simply knowing your market. You're pitching this idea to your neighbors. The challenge is to get them to buy into the idea of letting you have chickens in your backyard.

Before you rush out and say, "Howdy neighbor! We wanna have chickens! Are you cool with that?" you might want to consider how you're going to approach them about your unusual idea. Review the reasons why your neighbors might not want you to have chickens.

Chickens are smelly *– Your neighbor's experiences with chickens in the past occurred near large chicken farms where battery chickens are housed five in a cage, and wow, did they reek.*

Chickens are noisy – If your neighbors wanted to be awakened at 5 AM to the sound of a crowing **rooster**, they probably would have **chickens** of their own.

Chickens are messy – Your neighbors have seen stationary chicken pens where the chickens **run back and forth**, eating **all the vegetation** and making **a muddy, poopy mess**.

Mitzi and I addressed these questions with our **neighbors** before they even **thought** to ask. We created a **brochure** that outlined **Who, What, Why, When, Where, and How**.

To the right is **the** text of the **brochure** we created. We left **a** copy of this with every neighbor that we contacted.

After reading that, why wouldn't you want chickens in your neighborhood?

Notice that the brochure addressed all the major concerns **people would have** about chickens in the **area**. In the first **paragraph**,

---

Chickens at Magnolia Corner

According to the city ordinances, for health reasons we must notify each neighbor within 500 feet of our house that we intend to keep a small flock of laying hens on our family homestead. We have no plans for roosters.

We want to have Ameraucana hens. These are also known as "Easter Egg" chickens. They lay eggs that are green, blue, and sometimes pink. These medium sized birds are reliable layers, and are well-tempered and trusting.

Our chickens will be contained in a mobile coop called a chicken ark. As the chicken ark is moved around the yard, the birds have access to free range goodies like bugs, weeds, and worms. This creates a healthier bird and a tastier egg. The ark also eliminates the traditional problems of muddy, unhealthy chicken runs and smell.

We grow organic vegetables on our property that utilize rabbit droppings as the primary fertilizer. We compost our kitchen scraps and leaf litter, and collect rainwater for garden irrigation. We believe that raising chickens will assist our three daughters in developing mature and responsible behavior, as well as adding to the aesthetic quality, ease-of-maintenance, and best of all, taste of our vegetable garden.

If you have any questions, comments, or would just like to drop in and chat about our experiment in becoming more self-sufficient and ecologically friendly, please feel free to call either Dave or Mitzi Bissette at 556-5788.

they learned the city requires us to contact them, but that they will not be awakened early since there are no roosters.

We appealed to their since of curiosity in the second paragraph by telling them that we'll be raising "Easter Egg" chickens that are well-tempered and trusting.

The third paragraph eliminates any issues of smell and messiness, while the fourth paragraph makes an emotional appeal to anyone who has ever been a parent. Who would dare to disrupt an opportunity for children to develop mature and responsible behavior? Only a cretin would think of such a thing.

Lastly, we gave them our contact information. It's important for your neighbors to know that you trust them enough to provide them with a telephone number if they have any kind of problems with your rural activities in their urban environment.

Taking it to the Streets

We have a map of all the houses within 500 feet courtesy of Google. We have a brochure. Mitzi and I created a little form for the neighbors to sign that read:

Petition to the Town of Wake Forest for a Permit to Keep Livestock Near Residences. This permit request pertains to livestock to be kept at 230 S Main Street, Wake Forest, NC 27587

Code 1985 § 3-26, Section 6-52 -- Application: State the type and number of animals to be stabled, pastured, tied, or otherwise kept: Ameraucana laying hens to be kept in a small, mobile, non-fixed coop.

Code 1985 § 3-28, Section 6-54 Approval: Stabling, pasturing, tying or otherwise keeping of such animals in the place stated in the application will not endanger the health of any person occupying a dwelling house, apartment or residence within 500 feet of such place. Written assent to the issuance of the permit must be signed by one adult occupant of each dwelling, apartment, or other residence then occupied by human beings within 500 feet of the place the animals are to be stabled, pas-

tured, tied, or otherwise kept.

By signing the permit request below, you affirm that the keeping of a small coop of chickens at 230 S Main St, Wake Forest, NC will not affect the health and well being of you or your family.

Name	Address	Signature	Distance

We still received some minor objections that were easily answered and overcome. The most common question was, **"Why do you want chickens?"**

"Funny you should ask. I have put together a little brochure outlining the answer to that exact question. Do you have a few minutes to sit down and review it?"

One of our neighbors wanted to take a half hour or so to talk about his experiences with chickens when he was a young man. He told us that he had over 30,000 chickens and didn't mind a few around now.

We found that most of our neighbors were curious about chickens and some even excited about them. One neighbor, the fellow whose house is highly decorated for each and every holiday, including days like Veteran's Day and Valentine's Day, asked, "Would the coop would be visually pleasing?" Would it negatively affect his property value? After I showed him a 3D representation of the Catawba ConvertiCoops chicken ark I intended to build, he quickly signed off on the project.

In three hours we had all the signatures (and one verbal approval) that we needed to apply for our permit to keep domesticated foul.

Permitting

Applying for the permit with the town was easy. We ran into a small SNAFU when the permitting director noticed that we didn't have signatures from the owners of two of the vacant houses in the neighborhood. Mitzi argued the statute of the ordinance Section 6-54 reads that:

*Written assent to the issuance of the permit must be signed by one adult occupant of each dwelling, apartment, or other residence **then occupied by human beings**.*

Her point was that since neither of the dwellings were occupied by human beings, they were exempt from the requirements of the ordinance. The director agreed after consulting with the town attorney and we were issued a permit to keep chickens.

Changing the Ordinances

We receive walk-by visitors all the time at Magnolia Corner, our urban homestead. Sometimes our visitors leave wanting chickens of their own, but are put-off by the town's intentionally strict and bureaucratic permitting process. But not Emily...

After receiving a firm *No Chickens* from a kindly neighbor 450 feet away from her house, she decided to take advantage of our democratically elected republic style of government, and get the local ordinances changed!

Emily enlisted my assistance with the endeavor. We contacted several local news organizations, and were both frequently interviewed by our local news channel NBC17, The Wake Weekly, and The Raleigh News & Observer.

She started an educational blog. We both gathered petition signatures at the local farmers market. Emily began a local education program to teach people about the benefits of the keeping of urban chickens. She met individually with all of the town's commissioners to determine their positions on the situation

Emily submitted a written proposal to the town that offered a cap of 20 urban hens (no roosters) that had to be properly fenced, penned or otherwise contained. The town permitting office counter offered a maximum of 5 birds.

In a 4-1 vote by the Board of Commissioners, Wake Forest voted to allow homeowners to keep up to 10 chickens. The ordinance was passed!

Wake Forest Commissioners Vote In New Ordinance to Allow Urban Chickens in Town.

WAKE FOREST, NC. - The Town of Wake Forest's Town Board voted tonight to approve the chicken ordinance amendment. In a 4 to 1 vote, town commissioners ruled to append the town ordinances with an urban chicken amendment. The amendment allows for the keeping of up to ten chickens inside the town limits, excluding roosters.

Commissioner Thibodeau voiced concerns that the ordinance amendment was not restrictive enough. His concerns were that people would house the birds in their front yards and that there were no provisions for how the chickens were to be housed. Commissioner Drake reminded him that there were not provisions for the keeping of other pets like dogs and cats in the ordinances either.

The vote was taken after an open microphone discussion. Emily Cole addressed the board stating that she felt that the town's legal counsel proposal of five birds was too limited given the period of time that a chicken lays eggs verses it's lifespan. She then proposed that the amendment allow either ten or twelve birds. The assenting commissioners agreed to her proposal and increased the limit on urban chickens to ten.

"I'm very excited about this vote," said David Bissette, owner of the only permitted chickens inside the town limits.

Building the Chicken Ark

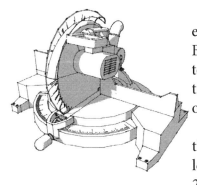

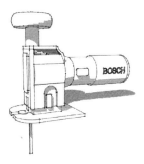

When I set out to design the Catawba ConvertiCoops DIY chicken coop, I did a lot of research into what I thought looked nice. The British have elevated backyard chicken coops, which they call an ark, to an art form. However, who wants to pay $1000.00 plus international shipping for a chicken ark? Not me! So I set out to build my own.

The chicken ark is based on a 30-60-90 degree triangle to make the math easier. Not that this math was easy for a numerically challenged person like myself. I used trigonometry for the first time in 20 years to build this coop. You won't have to use trig. I've already figured out the measurements for you. Isn't that why you purchased this guide anyway?

Tools

The precise angles of this chicken ark are difficult to cut without a miter saw. I went for years using a protractor and a circular saw to cut my angles. Never again. My wife picked up a De Walt miter saw at a yard sale for $25.00. It has changed the course (and tolerances) of my woodworking projects radically.

Since this is a triangle project, please ensure that you use those degrees exactly. Many miter saws have a detent at 31.62 degrees. Do not use that for cutting your 30 degree pieces. It's specifically used for cutting crown molding. Using the detent will throw off your measurements. I found this out the hard way on my first coop.

If you do not own a miter saw, I suggest checking eBay or Craigslist for a used saw. There's no need to purchase a new one just for this project when you can usually find a good used one just by asking around. Ask one of your neighbors when you're getting them to sign off on your chicken permit request. Perhaps your brother-in-law owns one?

Other tools that come in very handy are a table saw for making long straight cuts, a hand held jigsaw for making tight turns and the decorative handles, and an electric drill.

You can use a variety of fasteners for this project. My prototype chicken coop was built with wood screws After having built a coop using nails, I'm going to continue to recommend using screws. The nails began to pull out as the exposed wood aged .

If you build with screws, because you are using ¾" pieces of wood, consider pre-drilling your holes to keep the screws from splitting the wood. Once again, this is the voice of experience speaking.

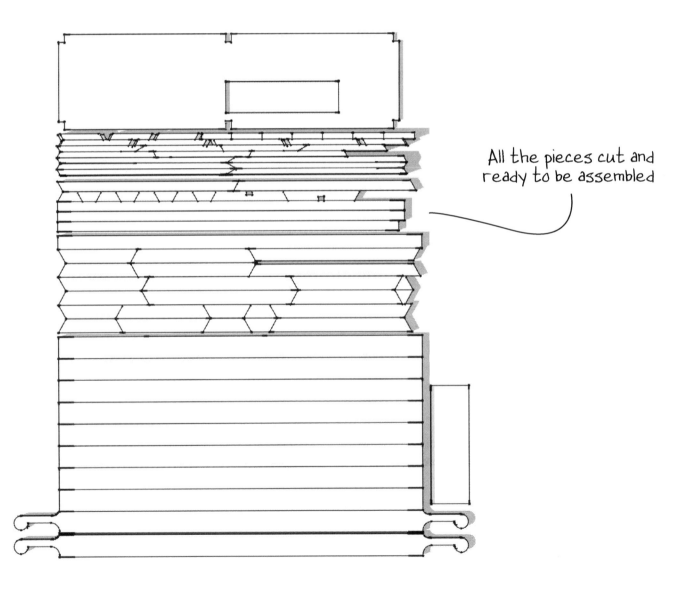

All the pieces cut and ready to be assembled

Materials List

Wood
- 2"x2"x8' furring strip x 8 boards
- 1"x2"x8' furring strip x 1 board
- 1"x3"x8' furring strip x 5 boards
- 1"x4"x8' furring strip x 6 boards
- 1"x4"x8' treated board x 1 board
- 1"x6"x8' treated board x 2 boards
- 1"x6"x8' treated or regular board x 6 boards
- 1"x6"x10' board x 2 boards
- 3/8" plywood 4'x8' x 1 board
- 1"x10"x shortest possible board

Hardware
- Garden gate latch x 4 (optional)
- Gate pull handle x 4
- 24" 3x2 Coated lawn fence x 50'
- Fence staples x 1 box
- 8 x 1¼" Wood screws x 1 box
- 8 x 2½" Wood screws x 1 box
- 3" Shallow depth door hinge x 2
- Wood glue

Pulley system
- 1/8" Galvanized cable x 10'
- Small pulley
- 1/8" Cable nut x 4
- 2" Eye hooks x 4

Furring strips are thin pieces of wood used to attach finished surfaces to wall studs. I've found that they work great for this project as well. So if you find wood with the dimensions stated above, you can bet that they are furring strips.

Cut List

2"x2"x8' furring strip x 8
- (3) 13" parallelograms for egg door legs,
  (7) 7+" rectangles for ramp rungs
- (4) 19¾" parallelograms for door legs,
  (1) 13" parallelogram for egg door leg
- (3) 26 1/8" trapezoids for under deck web member / ramp attachment mount
- (4) 30/60degree 23 3/16" trapezoids for nest box top chords
- (2) 30/60degree 47¼" trapezoid top chords
- (2) 30/60degree 47¼" trapezoid top chords
- (2) 30/60degree 47¼" trapezoid top chords
- (1) 63" for roost (trimmed to fit after assembly)

1"x3"x8' furring strip x 5
- (8) 6 ½" trapezoids for gusset plate,
  (2) 20½" trapezoids for roost support
- (2) 48" trapezoids for bottom chords
- (1) 90" rectangle for ridge line
- (1) 91½" rectangle for base side
- (1) 91½" rectangle for base side

1"x4"x8' furring strip x 6
- (1) 21 1/16" trapezoid for egg door
  (1) 33 7/16" trapezoid for coop door,
  (1) 45 1/16" trapezoid for coop door trimmed to 3" tall,
  (Caution: these cuts are going to be tight with no room for waste)
- (1) 21 1/16" trapezoid for egg door
  (1) 33 7/16" trapezoid for coop door,
  (1) 45 1/16" trapezoid for coop door trimmed to 3" tall,
  (Caution: these cuts are going to be tight with no room for waste)
- (1) 4 13/16" trapezoid for egg door
  (1) 24" trapezoid for threshold,
  (1) 29 7/16" trapezoid for coop door,
  (1) 41½" trapezoid for coop door,
- (1) 4 13/16" trapezoid for egg door
  (1) 24" trapezoid for threshold,
  (1) 29 7/16" trapezoid for coop door,
  (1) 41 1/2" trapezoid for coop door,

- (1) 8 13/16" trapezoid for egg door
  (1) 12 15/16" trapezoid for egg door,
  (1) 17 1/16" trapezoid for egg door,
  (1) 25 1/8" trapezoid for egg door,
  (1) 37 1/2" trapezoid for coop door
- (1) 8 13/16" trapezoid for egg door
  (1) 12 15/16" trapezoid for egg door,
  (1) 17 1/16" trapezoid for egg door,
  (1) 25 1/8" trapezoid for egg door,
  (1) 37 1/2" trapezoid for coop door,

(2) 1"x2"x8' furring strip
- Cut into two 3/4" strips (It's actually 1 1/2" wide). Ask the cutting station attendant at the home improvement center to assist you if you don't have a table saw or circular saw.

(2) 1"x6"x10' whitewood board
- Cut 12" decorative handles on each end

3/8" Plywood 4'x8'
- Cut to 90" long in store cutting station
- Cut in half to 24" wide in store cutting station

All trapezoids and parallelograms are 30 degrees unless otherwise noted. Please carefully review the plan illustrations before making your cuts.

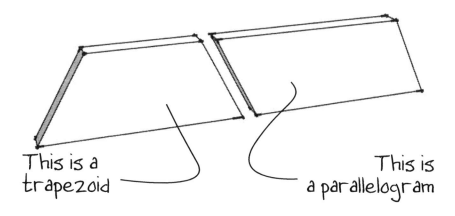

This is a trapezoid

This is a parallelogram

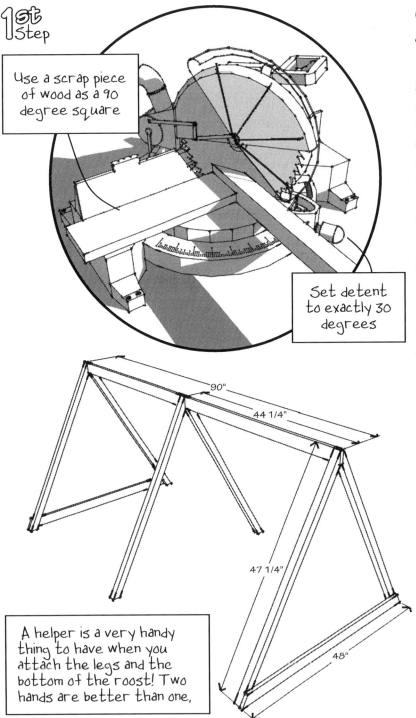

Go Build Yourself a Coop!

Cut 2"x2"x8' furring strips into six top chord coop legs measuring 47¼" in length along the longest side. One end should have a 30 degree cut and the other a 60 degree cut.

Sixty degree cuts require some finesse. Set your miter saw to 30 degrees. Using a piece of wood as a 90 degree square for the leg, make your 60 degree cuts first since your opportunity to make a miscut is significantly greater than with a 30 degree cut.

Cut a 1"x3"x8' furring strip 90" long to create a ridge board for the coop. Fasten the six 47¼" top chords to the ridge support. Fasten the middle top chords to the center of the ridge board 44¼" from each end.

Cut a 1"x3"x8' furring strip into two 48" (long side) bottom chords with 30 degree angles on each end.

Place the two 48" furring strip bottom chords at the end of both sides of the coop and attach at the base to tie the top chords together into a triangular truss shape.

Making and attaching the deck will probably be the most difficult part of this project for you. Get one of the associates at your home improvement store to cut down a piece of 3/8" 4'x8' plywood to 24"x90".

Use a jigsaw to cut six 2"x1½" rectangles from each end of the plywood and from the middle for the top chords.

Get a pencil and ruler / T-square to draw the ramp cut-out. Come in 15¾" from the end and 4" from the side, and draw a 30" x 8" rectangle. Cut out this rectangle using a circular saw or hand held jig saw. You'll need to drill a pilot hole to start the jig saw blade.

Cut three 26 1/8" pieces from 2"x2"x8' furring strip with 30 degree cuts at each end. These are web member supports for the deck of the coop. The middle brace will be the mount for the ramp the chicks use to get inside.

Measure 23 11/16" down from the top of the ridge board and mark your attachment spot. Person 1 lifts the deck and Person 2 attaches all three cross braces to the legs. Wood clamps come in very handy here if you don't have an assistant.

Alternative solution: Turn the whole unit upside down. Have your helper hold it then place the bottom board into the frame. Attach the three cross braces.

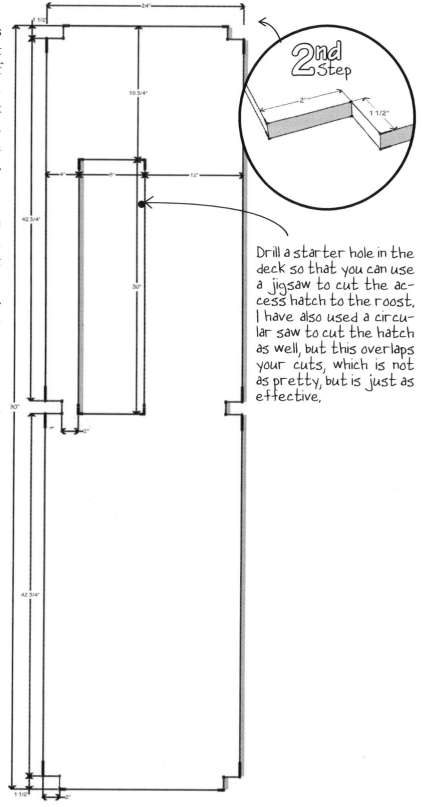

Drill a starter hole in the deck so that you can use a jigsaw to cut the access hatch to the roost. I have also used a circular saw to cut the hatch as well, but this overlaps your cuts, which is not as pretty, but is just as effective.

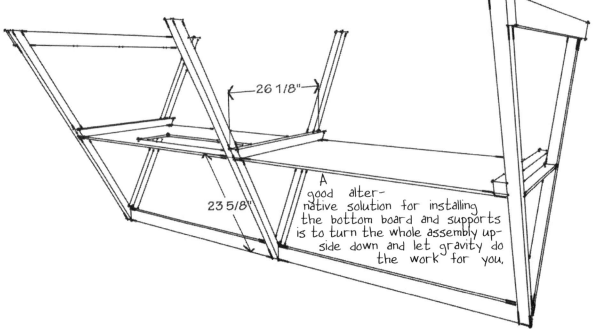

A good alternative solution for installing the bottom board and supports is to turn the whole assembly upside down and let gravity do the work for you.

3rd Step

It's time to begin the nest boxes. Get that miter saw ready. We're going to use it extensively for this step. Remember how to create 60 degree cuts? It's time to do it again. Cut four pieces from 2"x2"x8' furring strip so that the longest side is 23 3/16". Put a 60 degree cut on one end and a 30 degree on the other. Attach the nest box legs 12" in from the end legs.

In medieval times, people used threshed wheat and barley straw as a kind of carpet. They would put boards across the doorways to keep the threshing from being kicked out into the yard. The boards were called thresholds.

Cut two 24" (longest side) trapezoids from a 1"x4"x8' board with 30 degree

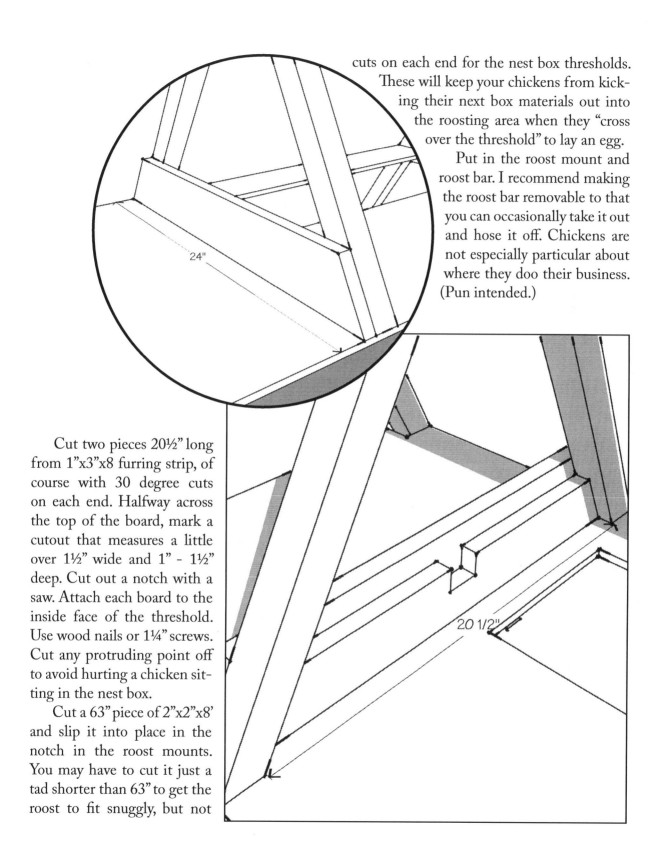

cuts on each end for the nest box thresholds. These will keep your chickens from kicking their next box materials out into the roosting area when they "cross over the threshold" to lay an egg.

Put in the roost mount and roost bar. I recommend making the roost bar removable to that you can occasionally take it out and hose it off. Chickens are not especially particular about where they doo their business. (Pun intended.)

Cut two pieces 20½" long from 1"x3"x8 furring strip, of course with 30 degree cuts on each end. Halfway across the top of the board, mark a cutout that measures a little over 1½" wide and 1" - 1½" deep. Cut out a notch with a saw. Attach each board to the inside face of the threshold. Use wood nails or 1¼" screws. Cut any protruding point off to avoid hurting a chicken sitting in the nest box.

Cut a 63" piece of 2"x2"x8' and slip it into place in the notch in the roost mounts. You may have to cut it just a tad shorter than 63" to get the roost to fit snuggly, but not

4th Step

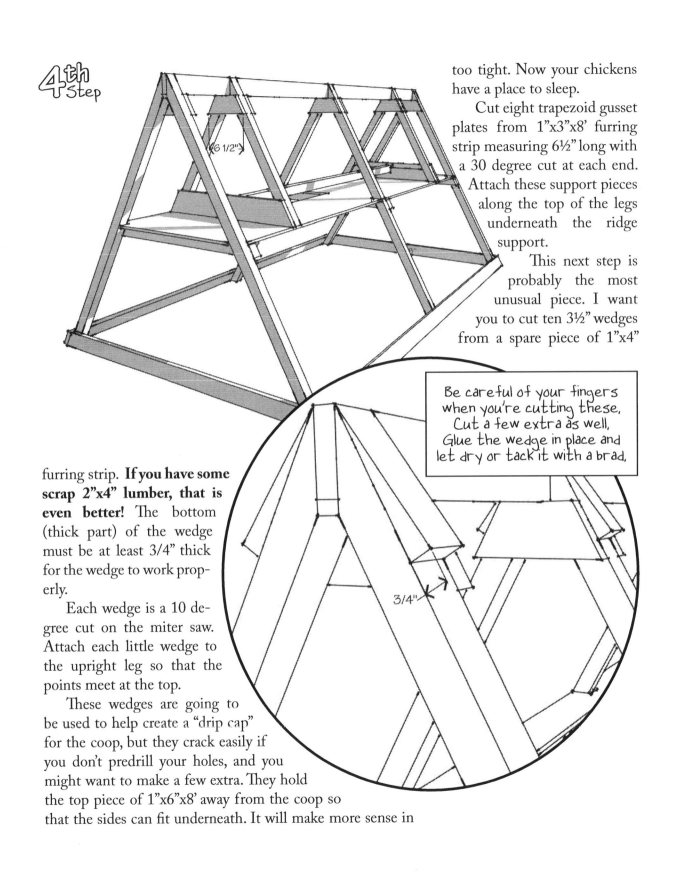

too tight. Now your chickens have a place to sleep.

Cut eight trapezoid gusset plates from 1"x3"x8' furring strip measuring 6½" long with a 30 degree cut at each end. Attach these support pieces along the top of the legs underneath the ridge support.

This next step is probably the most unusual piece. I want you to cut ten 3½" wedges from a spare piece of 1"x4" furring strip. **If you have some scrap 2"x4" lumber, that is even better!** The bottom (thick part) of the wedge must be at least 3/4" thick for the wedge to work properly.

Each wedge is a 10 degree cut on the miter saw. Attach each little wedge to the upright leg so that the points meet at the top.

These wedges are going to be used to help create a "drip cap" for the coop, but they crack easily if you don't predrill your holes, and you might want to make a few extra. They hold the top piece of 1"x6"x8' away from the coop so that the sides can fit underneath. It will make more sense in just a second.

It's time to put a roof on our coop. The roof consists of a piece of pressure treated 1"x4"x8' (or 1"x6"x8' for a wider weather cap) and two 1"x6"x8' pieces of treated board. Pressure treated lumber is a good idea, especially for the top board, since this area stays wettest the longest. Attach the top cap to the ridge board first with a 3" overhang on each side. Use the top cap board to line up your two side pieces.

Cut two 90" pieces of 24" tall 3"x2" vinyl covered lawn fence. Most of your local big box hardware stores carry this wire in the outside garden dept. It comes in lengths of 50'. You only require 15' of wire mesh for this project. Use the rest to build a chicken run.

After attaching the wire to the upright legs using fence staples and a hammer, cut two 91½" pieces of 1"x3"x8' furring strip. Attach them to the bottom of the legs. Screws are a good idea here.

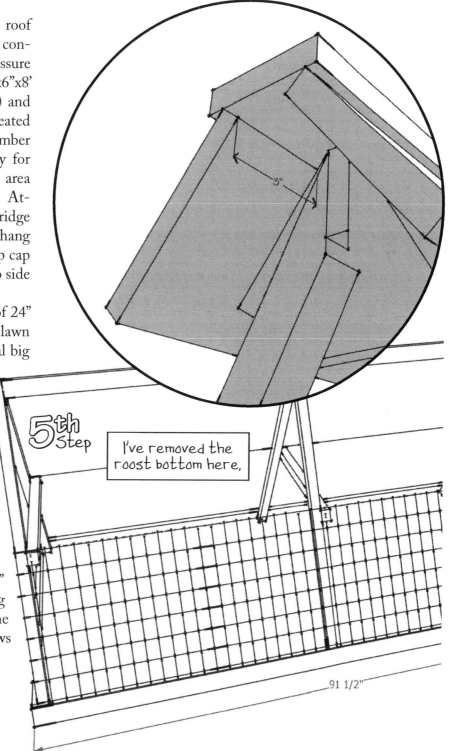

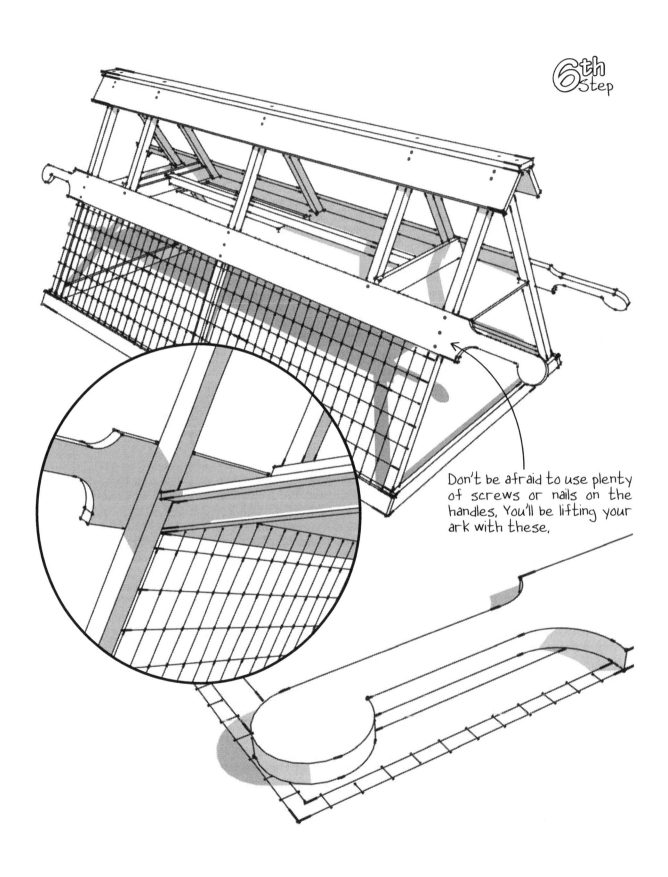

The handles are constructed from 1"x6"x10' boards. You will need two of them. You could put just attach the boards to the sides, but I find that the coop is much more attractive with a formal set of end handles.

Draw out a 12' long template and trace it onto the ends of the 10' pieces. Cut out your handles with a jigsaw. I also use a router on my handles to give them a smooth, round edge.

Attach the handles flush and level at the bottom with the cross bracing that holds the deck in place. Use lots of screws.

Create the removable sides from three pieces of 1"x6"x8' pressure treated or whitewood board. Overlap the boards by ¾" and glue, then screw the three pieces together.

I recommend pre-drilling your screw holes and using 1¼" wood screws to ensure your sides stay together permanently. Drill from the inside out (or top down as you see in the illustration). The 1¼" wood screws will not go all the way through 1½" of wood, and will not leave a hole for water.

Though seldom done, many people have trouble lifting this whole panel off the side of the ark. Some ark builders have chosen to saw it in half and use weather strip tape between the two panels

7th Step

Screw at least two handles on each side panel

8th Step

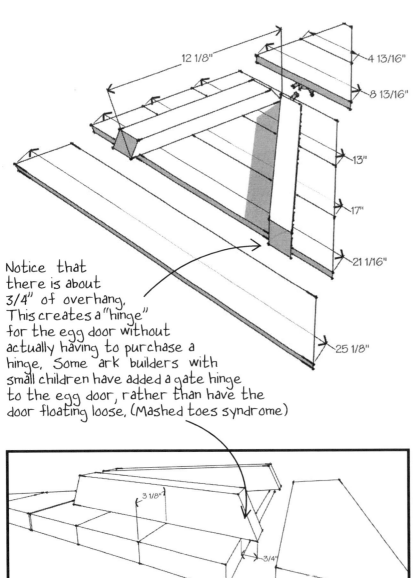

Notice that there is about 3/4" of overhang. This creates a "hinge" for the egg door without actually having to purchase a hinge. Some ark builders with small children have added a gate hinge to the egg door, rather than have the door floating loose. (Mashed toes syndrome)

We need to create some kind of a "lip" for the side panels so they can rest on the tops of the ark's handles. Use 1¼" wood screws to attach the two ¾" sawed pieces of 1"x2"x8' furring strip ¾" from the bottom of the side wall. Predrill all your holes and use 2 screws per foot, same as with the side boards.

Handles are recommended easily remove the sides for cleaning. I use two Stanley 11" heavy duty gate pulls on each side assembly set approximately 3' apart. You could also cut your own handles from a piece of 2"x2" scrap and attach them at a comfortable arms length apart on the outside of the door.

It's getting close to the end. All we have left is to add some ends to our coop! Each end set consists of two assemblies: an egg box door and a pen door.

The egg box doors are made of six trapezoids cut from 1"x4"x8' furring strip screwed to two 12 1/8" parallelograms cut from 2"x2"x8' furring strip.

Each of these measurements, once again, is a longest side measurement with 30 degree cuts on each end.

Cut two each of these boards, one for an egg door on

each side of the ark. Check the cut list at the beginning of the booklet. Screw through the front of the door into the 2x2s to ensure that your doors do not come apart.

Don't attach your egg doors to the chicken ark just yet. You need to build the run doors first. If you work from the bottom up, the spacing of the doors will allow for some weather expansion as your chicken ark is exposed to the elements.

The main coop doors are made in similar fashion using 2"x2" furring strips cut to 19 11/16" parallelograms for the door sup ports. Trim the 45 1/16" board to approx. 3" tall.

Cut two each of these boards, one for each coop door. Check the list at the beginning of the booklet.

I've given myself a little over an inch of overhang on the coop door rather that the 3/4" of the egg door since the coop door is heavier.

After assembling the door, you can used a variety of closing devices on the top. I use a small Stanley gate latch because I like the professional appearance. But a piece of wood with a screw will work just fine.

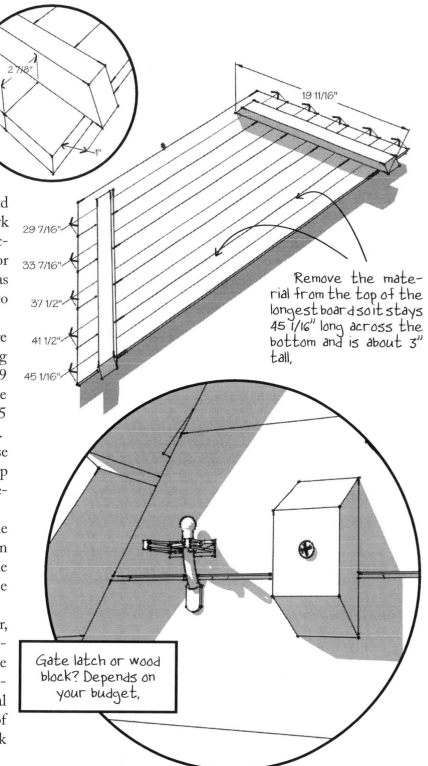

Remove the material from the top of the longest board so it stays 45 1/16" long across the bottom and is about 3" tall.

Gate latch or wood block? Depends on your budget.

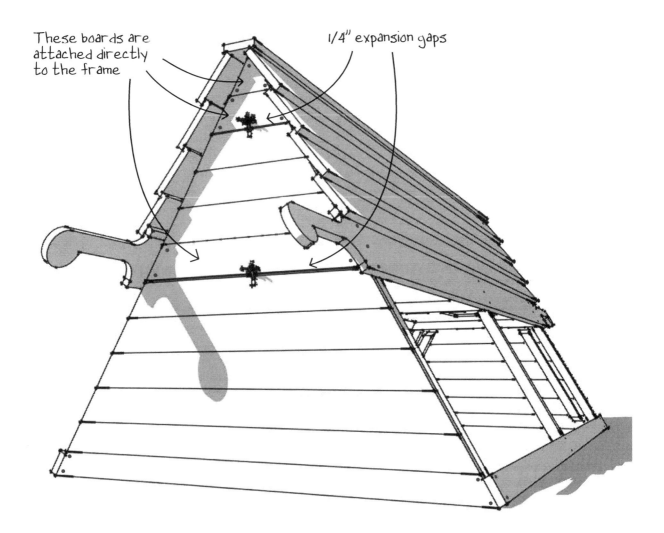

The last thing to do is crawl up underneath the coop to put in the ramp to the chicken's roost.

The ramp is made from a piece of 1"x10" cut to 30" long. Get the shortest piece you can find. No need to have a lot of waste. You will need to cut some of your 2"x2"x8' furring strip into 7"-8" or so strips. These will be the ladder rungs that the chickens use to climb into the roost. Attach the ramp to the deck support with the two 3" shallow depth door hinge. An easy way to access the area it is to turn the ark upside down again with the help of a friend.

The system to raise and lower the ramp is probably the piece I receive the most questions about. There are a hundred different ways to rig it, and everyone seems to want to do it differently. Here's how I do it:

Screw an eye hook into the last the ramp rungs towards the ground, then visually track up through the deck into the coop to a point directly above the eye hook.

Screw another eye hook into a top chord or gusset plate directly above the ramp. Create a small loop in the end of the 1/8" galvanized wire with enough overlap to attach two wire nuts. One wire nut may suffice, but two will ensure that your loop does not come undone.

Attach the loop to the ramp, then through the eye hook "pulley" and run it towards the end of the coop. The wire can be run out of the coop in the small gap between the side board and the egg door, or you can drill a 1/4" hole above the egg door catch and run the galvanized wire out of that. If you decide to drill the hole, put a washer on the end of the wire before making the handle.

Create another loop at the end of the galvanized wire for a handle and use a couple more wire nuts to finish the pulley system.

And there you have it! You have built the Catawba ConvertiCoops DIY Chicken Coop! Congratulations!

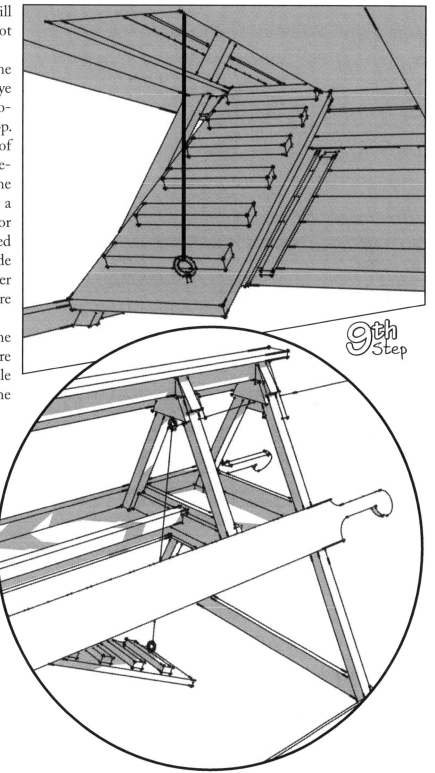

9th Step

Addendum

Upgrades and Suggestions

I have received many emails with suggestions for upgrading the Catawba ConvertiCoops chicken ark. I would like to take the opportunity to share some of the best ones with you.

"To make a nicer finished look make trim pieces to cover the legs where the chicken wire is stapled. These are pressure treated 2x2's ripped in half on the table saw, then tacked in place. They hide the staples and the cut ends of the wire and should make the wire more secure against being pulled off by predators."

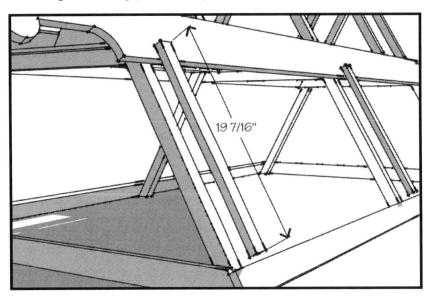

"For the 2x2's that touch the ground, use pressure treated wood if possible. I realize they don't sell pressure treated 2x2's, but you can cut a pressure treated 2x4 with a table saw and get a slightly larger piece of wood that can survive contact the ground longer."

"I love the simplicity of the wood door "hinges," but ended up putting metal hinges on the egg doors because my kids collect our eggs. I wanted no chance of one of them coming screaming with a broken foot because the egg door fell off."

"I was having a hard time getting the roof back on because of the angle plus weight. I cut one of the roof sides in two pieces and put extra handles on. It is much easier to manage now."

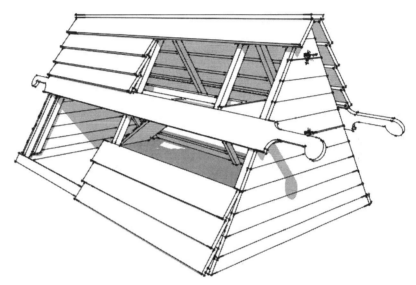

"I was having trouble with the chickens kicking their bedding out of the roost and down the ramp. I moved the roost over, and built a small retaining wall around the ramp entrance to keep them from kicking it out.

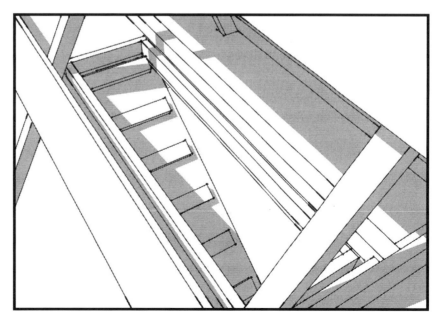

Frequently Asked Questions

How many chickens would this hold? - This is a comfortable 4 to 5 bird chicken coop for large breeds. It will hold 6 to 8 medium sized chickens based on the 4 sq feet per bird formula. That's a 2'x2' area. Measure that out with your hands and you'll see that their space requirements are minimal.

How do you keep your chickens warm in the winter? - Chickens are hardy. However, I would not recommend this type of coop for locations with lengthy, bitterly cold winters. Their waddles and combs get frostbitten. You'd want to build an completely enclosed "barnstyle" coop for those environments.

Occasional bitter cold is no problem for chickens. They are surrounded by a self adjusting, fully insulating, down sleeping bag across 90% of their body. I would use the other half sheet of the plywood you purchased to cover the windward side of the coop's run. Leave the leeward side open for light and ventilation.

You can run an 100w light bulb out to the coop. I had 25 pullets in a Catawba ConvertiCoop that were born in October and were beginning to feather out (lose their fluffy down feathers). Temperatures at night have dropped below 20 degrees F and the birds were fine with a light bulb for warmth.

How do you defeat predators? - Completely enclosing the lower run (including the floor) in a smaller mesh could do the trick. You could use a smaller 1x2 welded/galvanized mesh on the sides. This is the same kind of wire mesh I make my rabbit cages from and can be purchased by the roll from Bass Rabbit Supplies or Klubertanz.

Personally, I like 2x3 green vinyl coated garden wire. It doesn't chew up my hands when I'm working with it like the uncoated stuff does. Rather than choose a smaller mesh, I recommend a dual prong approach to predator control.

First put down a layer of twisted chicken wire. This is not to keep critters out, but to keep the chicken's heads inside. If a chicken pokes its head out of the run while a raccoon is prowling about, POP... now you've got Mike the Headless Chicken! Over top of that, put a layer of the 2x3 wire to keep the predators out.

Are the plans easily modified to make the coop larger? - Of course, if by larger you mean longer. You can purchase any length of wood you desire with little modification. If you want it wider than 4 feet, well... that will require extensive modification and the recalculation of practically every dimension.

This coop will accommodate up to 8 smaller chickens based on the 4 sq feet per bird formula. Each additional foot in length that you increase the coop will allow space for another bird.

Are two nest boxes enough? - All my chickens seem to want to lay in the same next box. One will be full and the other will be empty. Two nests are a gracious plenty. The industry standard for free-range egg production is one nest box for every ten birds. Chickens will seek out an enclosed, quiet, dark place to lay their eggs.

I am interested in what the approximate cost of the chicken ark would be. - Approx materials costs, due to the fact that this is a wood structure, is between $175 - $225 depending on your locale... and your cost-conscious shoppability. I have no qualms in playing the Big Box home improvement centers against each other with their Cost + 10% Guarantees.

How easy is the "upstairs" to clean? - Simple. Just line the roost area with a thick layer of newspaper. Make sure you remove any glossy circular inserts. When you are ready to clean it, take off the sides and roll up the newspaper. That can then go into the compost bin.

What do you suggest to use with your design as a feeder? - I use a standard 3.5 gallon hanging feeder from Tractor Supply with this unit. I hang the feeder and waterer in the run area using screw in hooks.

Can you move the coop without harming the chickens or do we wait until later when they are roosting? - Of course! They'll just kind of walk along underneath the coop. Just don't lift the ark so high up that they can run out from underneath. We've done that before when moving it over some rocks. When that happens, if your birds are a little on the wild side, you just have to wait for them to come back to the coop to roost that evening. Make sure you leave the door open for them.

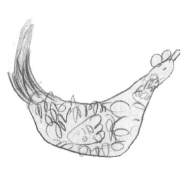

Chicken drawing by our youngest daughter Sarah at age 5

Can you share your "maintenance" routine and what you use for keeping the coop in tip-top shape? - Give your coop a few exterior coats of boiled linseed oil. BLO has been used for many many years as a sealant and wood preservative. The US Army used BLO of the stocks of firearms in WWII... that's how great the stuff is. **Do not get raw linseed oil.** Boiling changes the structure of the oil molecule and makes it into a polymer.

Line the roost area with a thick layer of newspaper. When it is soiled, you can roll it up and put it in the compost bin or the trash can. We do this once a week or so. Just keep fresh straw in the nestbox and you should be fine there.

Move the coop 4' to the left or right every couple of days to give your chickens fresh forage.

Husbandry

Feeding and watering your chickens is a lot different from feeding a cat or dog. Chickens are more self sustaining, and don't require the same kind of attention that other caged animals require. You can free range your chickens and they will find about 1/4 of their food in the wild. They're opportunistic feeders and eat practically anything; bugs, slugs, worms, weeds and grass.

Plants in your garden are all fair game to the ravages of these natural scratching cultivators. One thing that is not always available is a source of fresh, clean water.

There are several brands of automatic waterer available. There are double walled galvanized steel founts that hold a couple of gallons of water and need to be checked every morning. There are waterers that attach to a garden hose. Which one you use depends on how far away from the house you keep your coop, and how many feet of garden hose you want to purchase. I like to move my chickens all over the place, so I use the old fashioned manual waterer. I've hung it with a couple of 2" eye hooks underneath the nest box, screwed into one of the deck supports.

There are a several of brands of automatic waterer that I would recommend. The Blitz Auto-Wata (even though it's blue plastic... ugh!) is a good solution to providing fresh water to your birds. You can screw it directly into inside of the coop door at the chicken's head height. These run $15 - $23 online.

The Plasson plastic automatic watering system is a gravity fed system that can provide your chickens with 5 gallons or more of water. This product is used extensively throughout the poultry world for supplying poultry with fresh water. It's rounded top makes it impossible for the birds to perch on top of the watering device and get poo all in the water.

Grown chickens eat one of two things, other than

your garden; chicken scratch or laying mash. Chicken scratch is a lot less expensive since it's made of cracked grains... mostly corn. Laying mash isn't really mash like we know it. It's not wet and squishy. It's a dry pelletized product that is high in protein and other stuff that agriculturalists have determined that your chickens need once they start a-layin'. We use a galvanized 3.5 gallon chicken feeder. We're not big fans of plastic at Magnolia Corner.

Speaking of laying, my Rhode Island Reds produce one egg for every 14 hours of sunlight they receive. During the summer, that's every day. During the winter, every other day or so.

Why Not Start Your OWN Informal Chicken Coop Business?

I've fielded several questions recently from people who either want to go into business with me selling plans (*http://affiliate.catawbacoops.com*) or asking permission to start selling their own coops based off my plans. Here's what I have to say about that, "GO FOR IT! This is America baby, land of the free and home of the brave. This is the country of Free Enterprise."

With all the garbage economic policy coming out of Washington DC, a lot of people are scared about losing their jobs, as they should be. Our country was not founded on the concept of servitude to a boss in return for pieces of green paper. America's greatness stemmed from the ability of its inhabitants to recognize a market niche, make a job for themselves, and maybe with some time and moxy, create a fully fledged business out of their endeavors.

America once had localized economies. A farmer took his corn to the miller, who in turn sold to the baker, who sold to the blacksmith who, in return shoe'd the baker's horse. That same horse was loaned back to the farmer to plow his fields the upcoming spring, since the farmer's plow horse was going to foal soon. See how that works?

Sure, fiat currency in the form of Federal Reserve Note dollars helped simply the exchange of goods and services. But each transaction was supported by a tangible... something that could be seen, felt, or held.

I'm about to spill the beans on retail. Even if you've worked in retail, you may not have heard about the retail keystone. It works this way. If I am a retailer who sells shirts to the public, I try to run my business on a 50% profit margin. That means that my cost will be 50% of that price which I sell the shirt to you.

For instance, if I sell a shirt in my store for $20.00, my cost to purchase that shirt from the manufacturer/distributor is generally going to be ±$10.00. In other words, I marked up the shirt 100% so that I could sell it for twice what I paid for it. What a racquet! I have a gross profit of $10.00 a shirt! If I sell 100 of them a week, I've made $1,000.00, right?

Wrong my friend! **I own a retail establishment.** From my $10.00 that I made on the sale I have to remove my fixed costs; expensive commercial building rent, electricity, internet, and phones, as well as operational costs like paying employees and their health insurance, inflated labor union rates, unemployment benefits, etc.

After all is done, I may have $2.00 left over from the sale to pay myself. I must sell 100 shirts a week just to make a $200 paycheck (net profit). But I miscalculated the market and people's tastes in shirts. I have to mark down my shirts 30% to sell them, now giving me a 20% profit margin. But I still have fixed and operational costs to cover before I take a paycheck this week. Actually, I'm not taking a paycheck this week. Welcome to the state of Formal Business In America™.

If you have a few minutes read an amazing blog at OfTwoMinds.com by author Charles Hugh Smith entitled "End of Work, End of Affluence III: The Rise of Informal Businesses."

Smith writes,

Even in high-tech, wealthy Japan, tiny businesses abound. Wander around a residential neighborhood and you'll find a small stall fronting a house staffed by a retired person selling cigarettes, candy and soft drinks. Maybe they only sell a few dollars' worth of goods a day, but it's something, and in the meantime the proprietor is reading a magazine or watching TV. Fixed costs of these thriving enterprises: a small fee to some authority, an old cart and umbrella--and maybe a battered wok or ice chest.

So this is what I envision happening as the Recession drives standard-issue high-fixed cost "formal" enterprises out of business in the U.S.

- *The mechanic who used to tune your (used) vehicle for $300 at the dealership (now gone) tunes it up in his home garage for $120--parts included.*
- *The gal who cut your hair for $40 at the salon now cuts it at your house for $10.*
- *The chef who used to cook at the restaurant that charged $60 per meal now delivers a gourmet plate to your door for $10 each.*
- *The neighbor kids' lemonade stand is now a permanent feature; you pay 50 cents for a lemonade or soft drink instead of $3 at Starbucks.*
- *Used book sellers spread their wares on the sidewalk, or in fold-up booths; for reasons unknown, one street becomes the "place to go buy used books."*
- *The neighborhood jazz guy/gal sets up and plays with his/her pals in the backyard; donations welcome.*
- *The neighborhood chips in a few bucks each to make it worth a local Iraq War vet's time to keep an eye on things in the evenings.*
- *When your piece-of-crap Ikea desk busts, you call a guy who can fix it for $10 (glue, clamps, a few ledger strips and screws) rather than go blow $50 on another particle board desk which will bust anyway. (oh, and you don't have the $50 anyway.)*
- *The couple with the carefully tended peach or apple tree bakes 30 pies and trades them for vegetables, babysitting, etc.*

Here is the contents of an email I wrote recently to a gentleman from southern California who contacted me about getting into the chicken coop business.

"What I recommend to you is this: Buy a set of the plans and use those to go into business for yourself. Get some used tools on eBay or Craigslist. Build one ark in your garage and use it as practice... maybe something to keep your chickens in. Build a second one and don't let your birds near it. This one is going to be your display coop. Promote your business locally and sell custom chicken coops in your city or neighborhood. Charge 1/2 up front (to cover your material's cost) and then the rest upon delivery.

This way, your max out of pocket expenses are maybe $100 worth of tools and $350 worth of materials to start your business. Heck, you can't get into an MLM business for that cheap[1]... and this will truly be a business of your own."

Whatever you do, maybe now is the time to diversify yourself. Don't wait for the hatchet to drop on your job before you start something else. My booklet might be copyrighted, but the coop is not. Could this be the business for you as well?

P.S. If you do start a business selling these coops, how about a $20 Paypal donation to *catawbacoops@gmail.com* for each Catawba ConvertiCoop sold? This is on the honor system of course, but it's always appreciated.

Additional Reading

Some books that I have found beneficial on husbandry or wifery of chickens are:

- **Storey's Guide to Raising Chickens (Paperback - Jan 12, 1995)**
- **Chickens In Your Backyard: A Beginner's Guide - Rick & Gail Luttmann (Paperback - Sep 15, 1976)**
- **Backyard Poultry Magazine - 145 Industrial Drive, Medford, WI 54451, Phone: 715-785-7979**

---

[1] Yes, I know the costs of most MLM business business kits are not $450... but once you add in motivational organization costs like standing order tapes, leadership weekends, weekly meeting room rentals, and transportation to and from, it gets expensive quickly unless you sell a lot of soap. Now I like soap just as much as the next man, but I like chickens a lot better. I eat more eggs than I use dish detergent.

Downloadable information

I've created a download file full of support materials for you as well. I'm going to give you access to a Sketchup 3D tour I created so that you can see the coop on your computer. Send an email to *catawbacoops@gmail.com* and put the words *DIY SKP* in the title of your email.

The 3D renders in this booklet were created by a fine product from Google called Sketchup. You can download Sketchup from *http://sketchup.google.com*.

I've made a neat little animated tour of the construction of the coop that you can access by clicking the tabs at the top of the Sketchup Viewer screen.

Thank you for purchasing my DIY Chicken Ark Plans. Best wishes for your new family flock of chickens. If you have any additional questions, please feel free to send them to the email address above. I try to check my email at least once a day.

Kindest Regards,

Coop Gallery

Here are some coops as created by people who have already purchased these plans.

Dave's Prototype Coop

This is my original. There are some things I don't like about it, such as horizontal boards placed along the ground that catch all kinds of dirt that the chickens kick around. I fixed these issues with the Catawba ConvertiCoop.

Catawba ConvertiCoop "Final Edition"

This is my second coop. I used the prototype to work the kinks out and then built this one based solely upon the plans.

Deniece is the first person to send me pictures of her completed coop. She has a word of advice for future coop builders:

"I have the egg and coop doors done on one side. Unfortunately, I'm fighting board warping, so that's making it difficult. I think I'm going to build the other side by getting the wood close to the right size, but a little oversize. I'll then trim it down to the right size using my band saw. That will make cleaner matching edges."

Ricky's mom writes, *"My 15 year-old son finished the coop in just a couple days. He has never built anything before in his life and did great! It looks even better than the photos. He has stained/sealed it and it looks like a high end piece of furniture. I am sure he will have no trouble getting the price he wants for it... if he can let it go! Thanks again for the great customer support."*

Laura was having some difficulties putting the panels on her coop. She writes, "*I was having a hard time getting the roof back on because of the angle plus weight. We cut one of the roof sides in two pieces and put extra handles on, and it is much easier to manage.*"

I think this is an excellent idea for someone who may not be able to handle the full weight of one of the sides. The small gap could be filled with a weatherproof gasket like those found on the bottom of screen doors.

Jill was one of the first people to purchase coop plans from me. She says that "nothing comes between a man and his chicken!"

Made in the USA
Lexington, KY
11 January 2011